FISHING! #@%&*!

Cartoons by John Troy

FISHING! #@%&*!

Cartoons by John Troy

Nick Lyons Books
31 West 21 St.
New York, NY 10010

Printed in the United States of America

10   9   8   7   6   5   4   3   2   1

Library of Congress Cataloging-in-Publication Data

Troy, John.
  Fishing! : cartoons.

  Title followed by "@%&*!."
  1. Fishing—Caricatures and cartoons.   2. American wit and humor, Pictorial.   I. Title.
NC1429.T695A4   1985a   741.5'973   86-1413
ISBN 0–941130–10–X

"How nice, my husband is an ardent fisherman too."

"I like to think there's a lunker in every pool I fish."

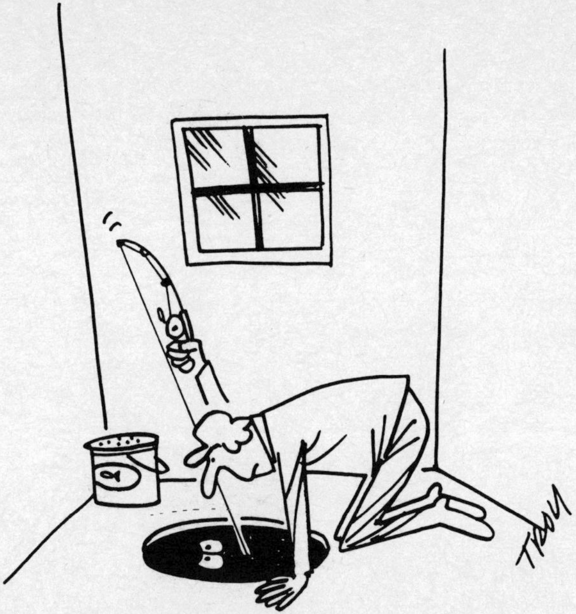
TROY

"Don't let me catch you spawning again!"

"If it's all the same to you, I'll get off at the next tip-up."

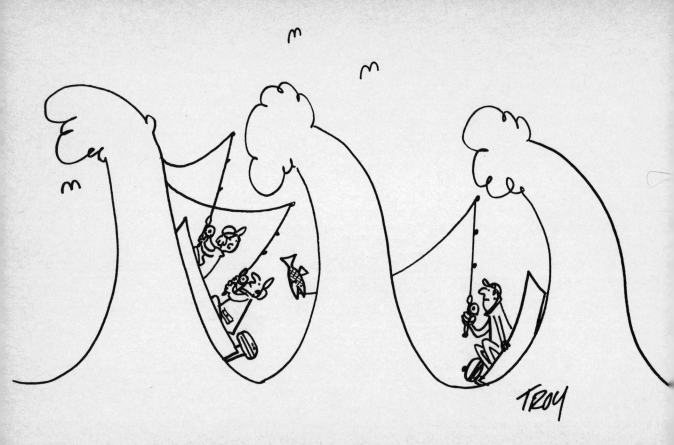

"Tell the man in the next boat he has a fish on."

"That salmon made a 200-foot run, which would have been the thrill of a lifetime except I only had 90 feet of line."

"Did you ever see a spawning run like this one?"

"This is the last time *you* plan our fishing trips."

"Fetch! Fetch!"

"She likes to go with me, but really doesn't care that much for fishing."

"I just can't get them interested in fishing."

"Excuse me, I couldn't help noticing that you're fly fishing."

"Look at that nut fishing in this weather."

"This must be a good place to eat, look at all the fishermen here."

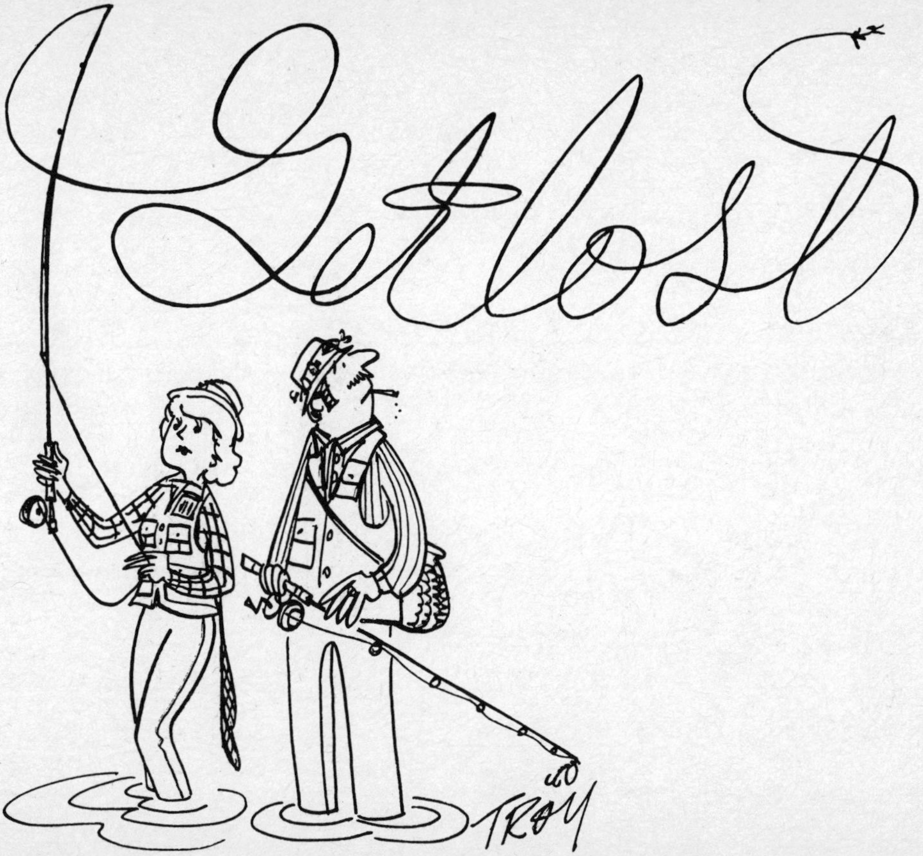
Get lost
TROY

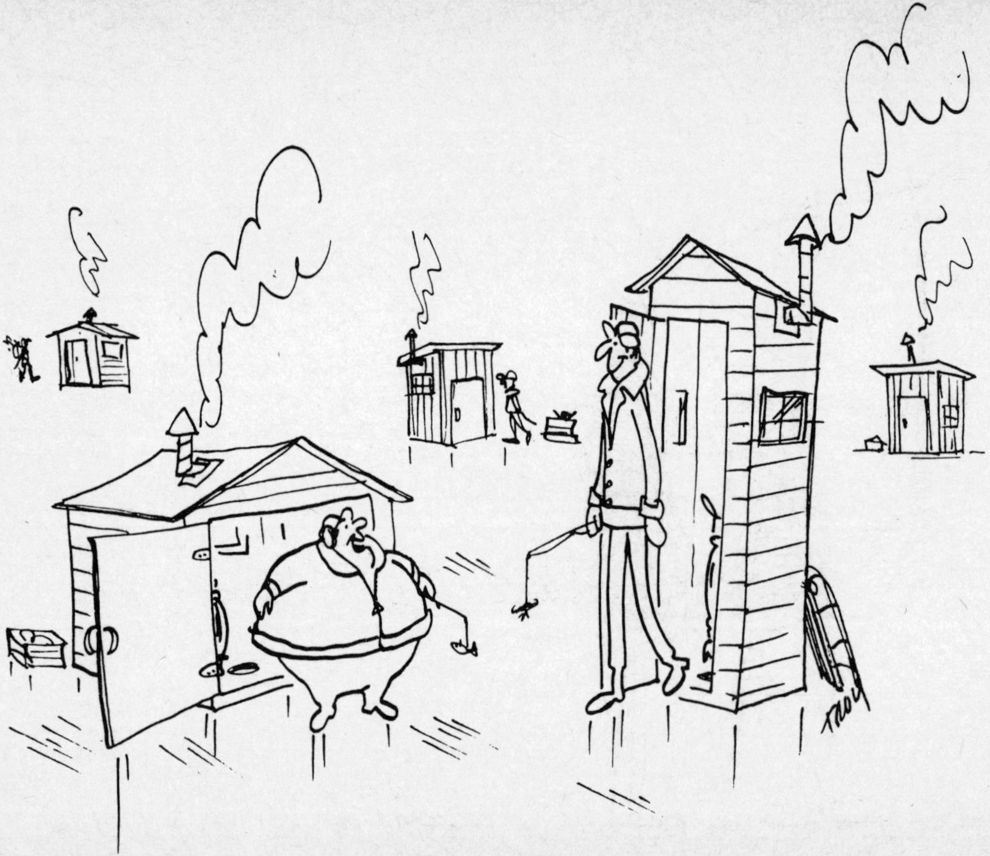
TROY

"How they biting?"

"... and a seafood platter for my friend."

"Thirty dozen shiners. Wow, what are you fishing for, whales or something?"

"This is our top-selling catfish bait—Eau de Entrails."

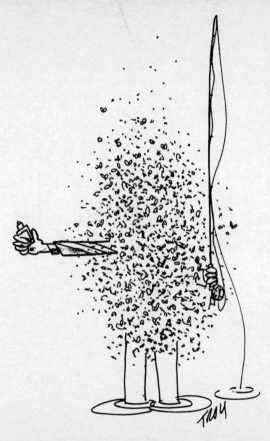

"Here, need some insect repellant?"

"Just what I always wanted, son, a magforce 12-foot Powercasting Surfbuster."

"I'm no good until I have my morning toxic waste."

"We'll look back on this some day and laugh."

"Tom landed a musky today. Without a net."

"Henry, don't forget to ask George about his fishing trip."

"No, my flotation jacket is *not* inflated."

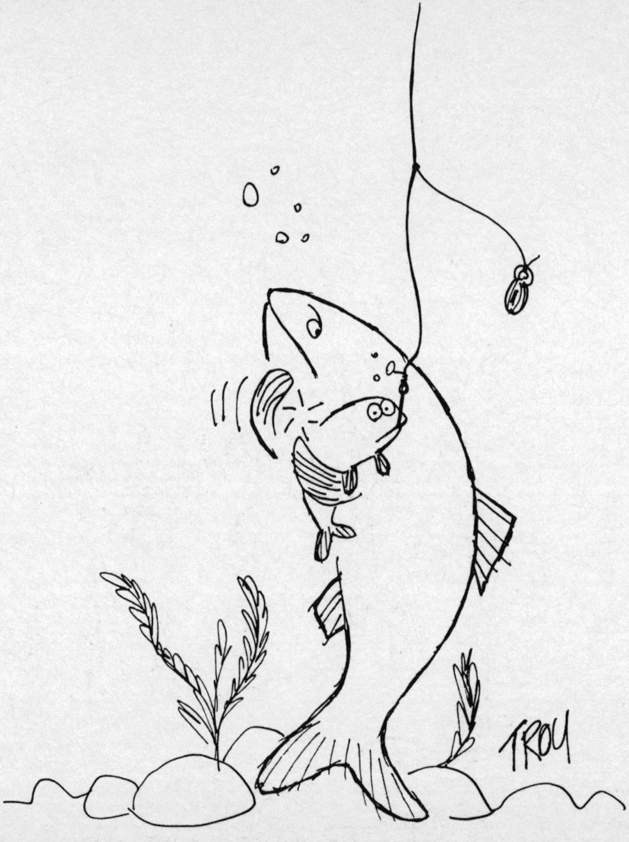
TROY

"Couldn't you just show them the pictures?"

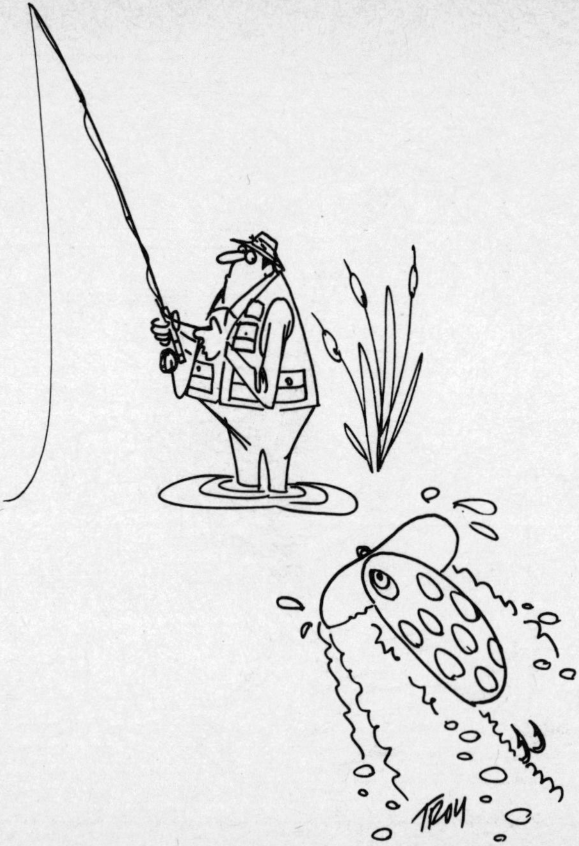
TROY

"Does this stream have a slippery bottom?"

"When are you going to take that musky out of the bathtub?"

"When you said you wanted to show me a good hooker, I thought . . ."

"Have you ever thought of becoming a fly fisherman?"

"Once in a while an alligator will follow the lure right up to the boat."

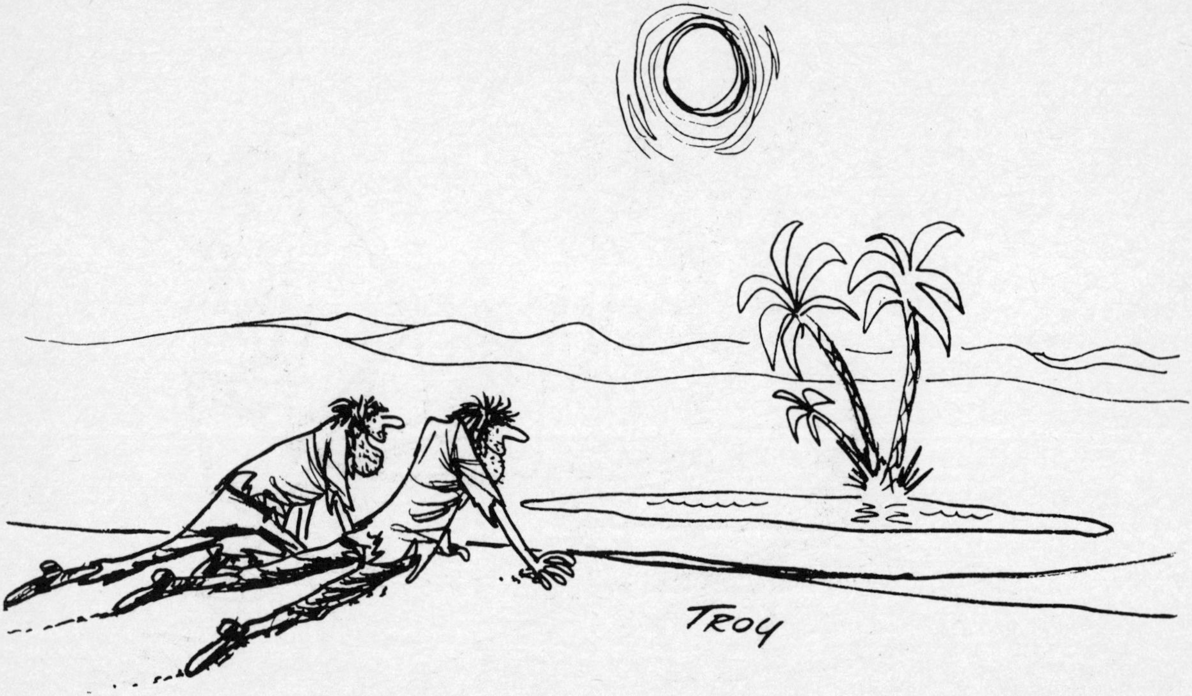
TROY

"See any rises?"

"I know these trout are hard to sneak up on, but this is ridiculous."

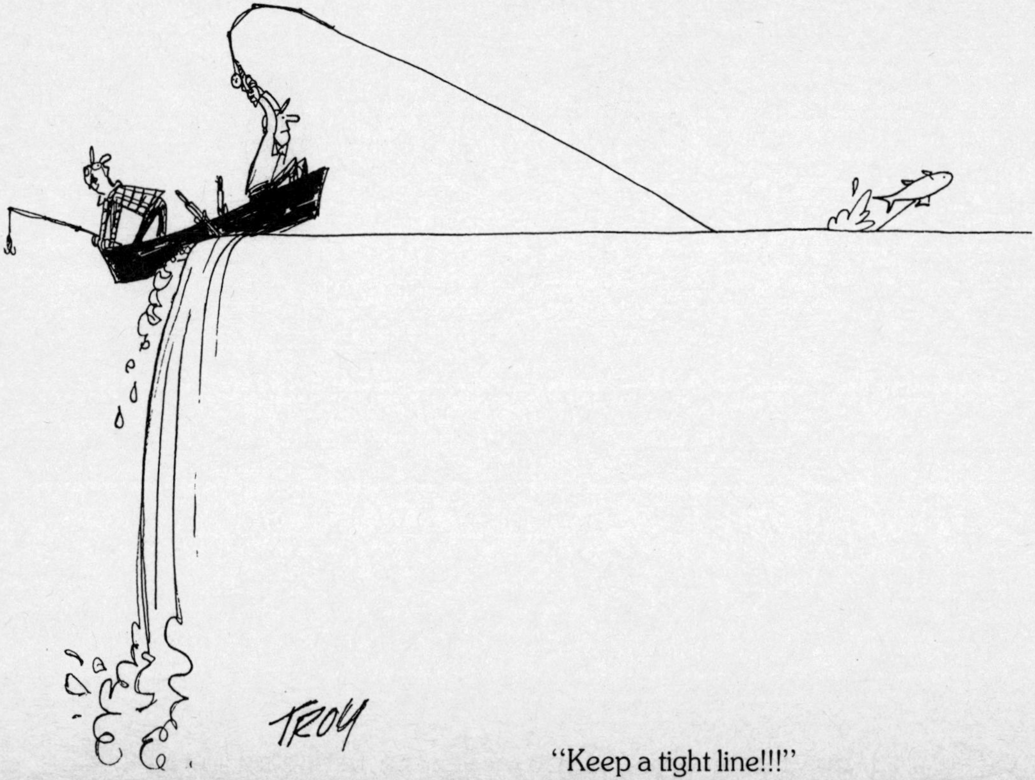
TROY

"Keep a tight line!!!"

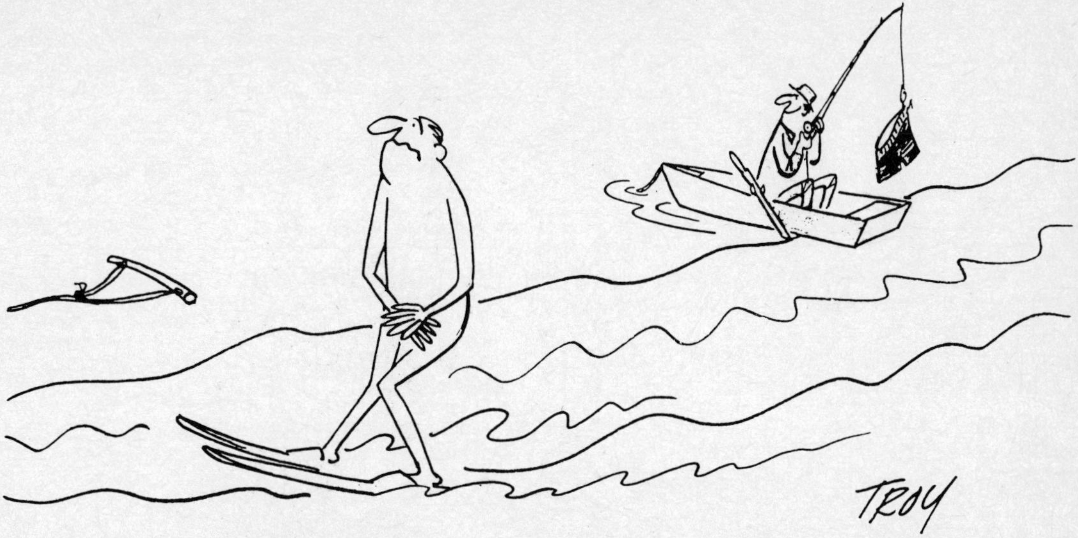
TROY

"It's a good thing our ice-fishing gear is in the trunk or our day would *really* be spoiled."

"You wanna talk backbone in a rod . . ."

"Did you see that one jump?"

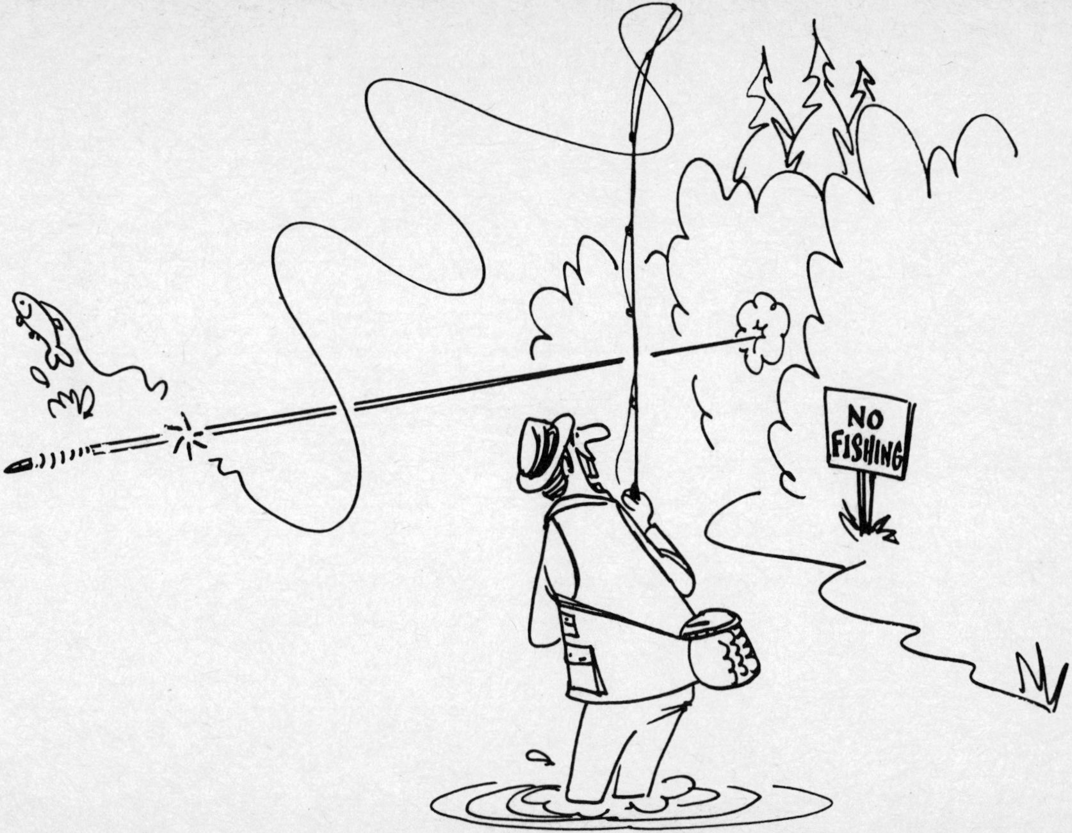
NO FISHING

"Whoa, sorry, I didn't see the sign!"

"What's he doing that we're not doing?"

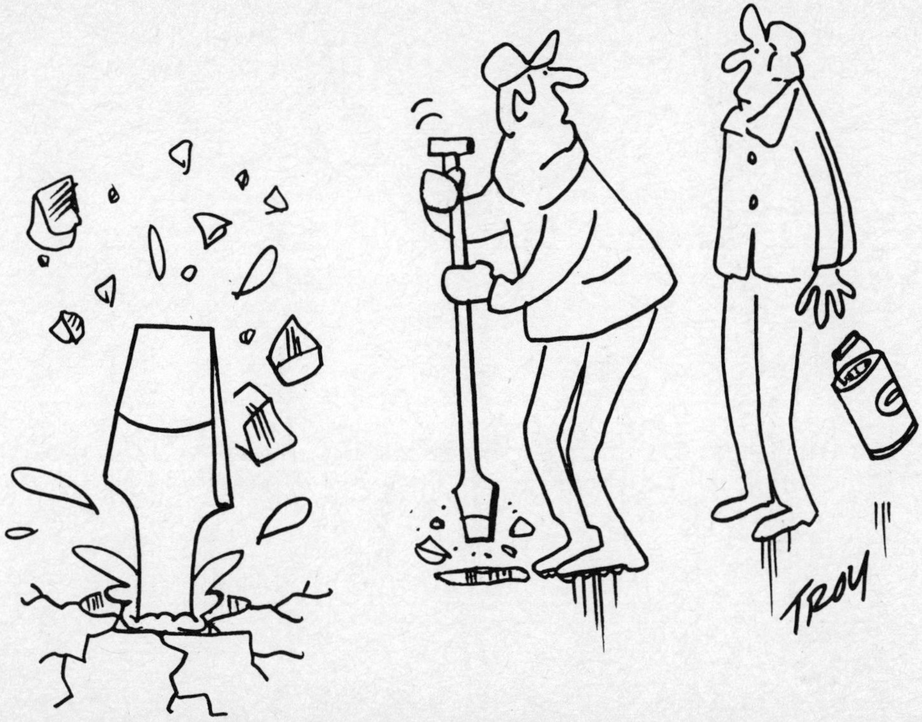
TROY

"Uh-oh."

"Hey, Judy baited her own hook!"

"Who are you to tell me there's no bass in this stream?"

"Control yourself, Peasly, when they don't hit on flies, *they don't hit on flies*— it's all part of the game!"

"Really into ultralight, aren't you?"

"Quick, caddy, my eight-foot graphite with a 5X tippet!"

"Yessir, these South American streams are teeming with fish—bass, trout, snook, tarpon, piranhas . . ."

"Well, has my casting improved?"

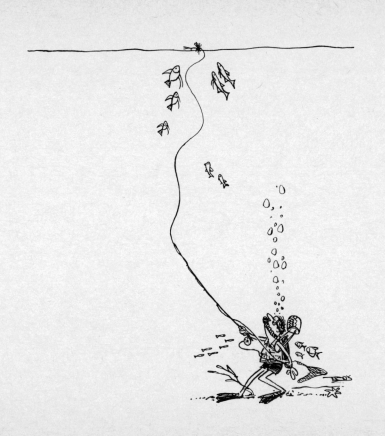

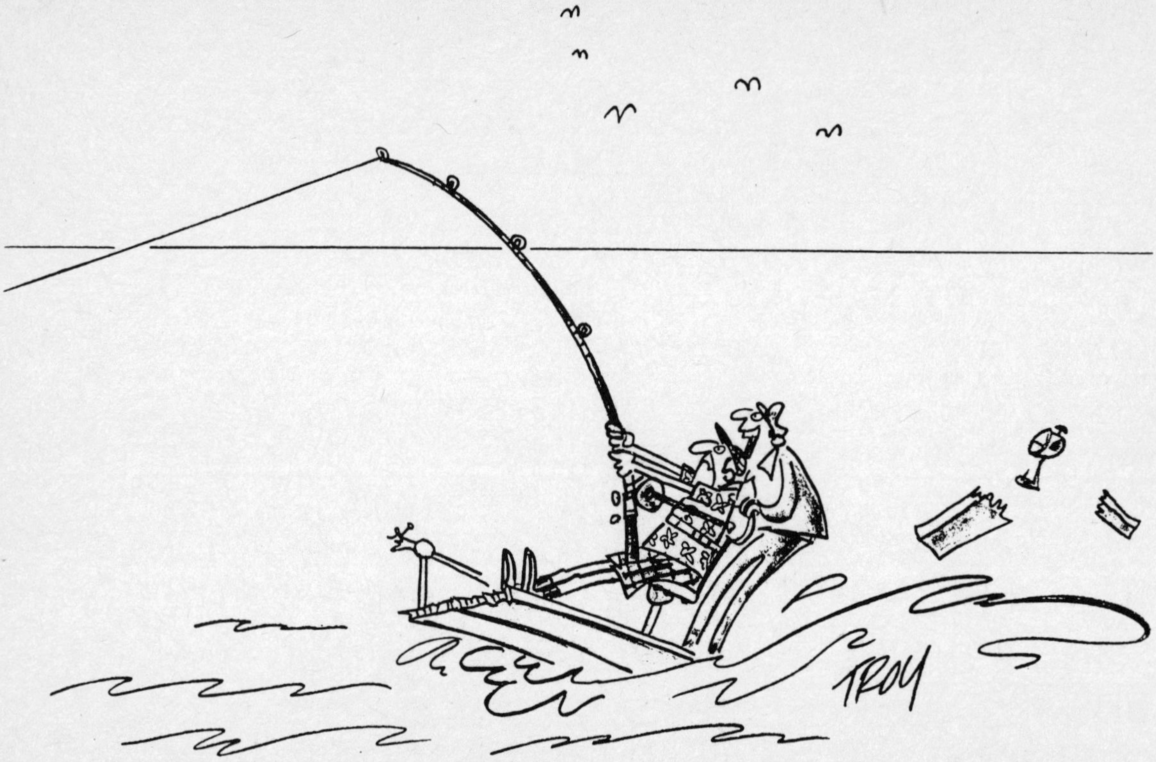
TROY

"I think he's tiring!"

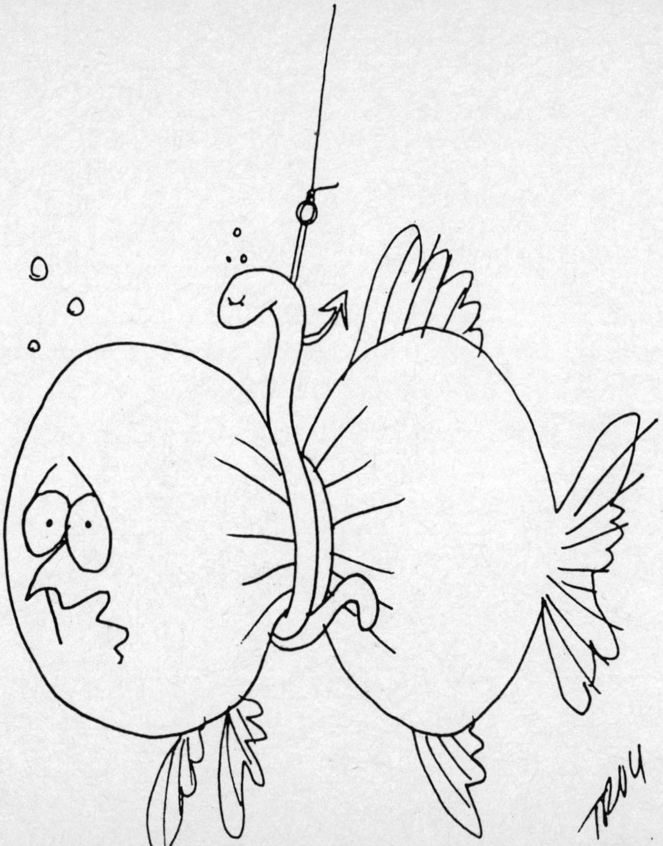
TROY

"I hear you're into ice fishing."

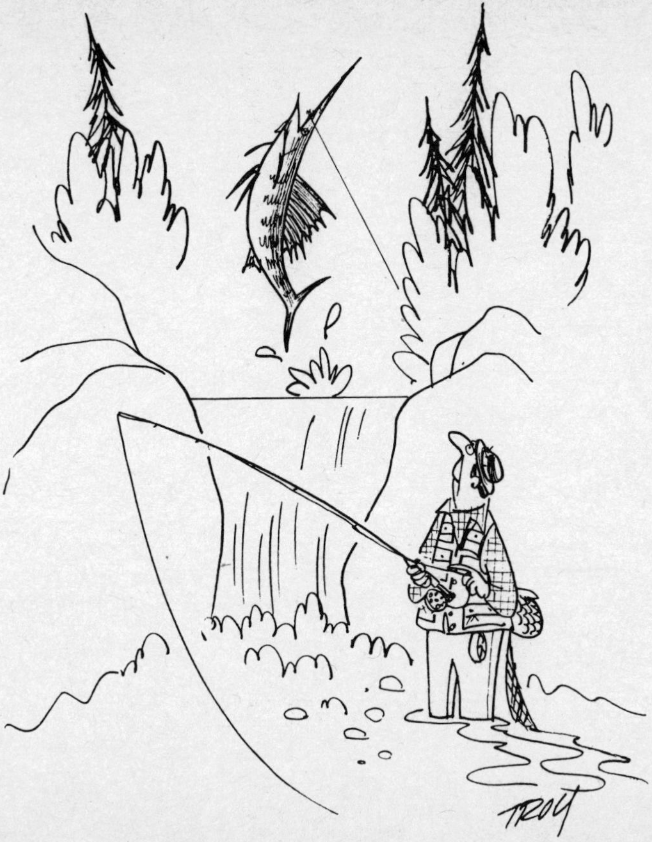
TROY

"I got one!"

"So *that's* how he reaches those offshore blues."

"If you don't mind, I think I'll go ahead."

"You want a real fish taker? Garden hackle, that's what!"

"He loves to fish, but he's only so-so on hunting."

"I don't go for that sissy tackle!"

"Ice fishing season is never quite long enough for Edgar."

"Ah, my very own graphite rod."

"This must be the 'Trophy Stretch.'"

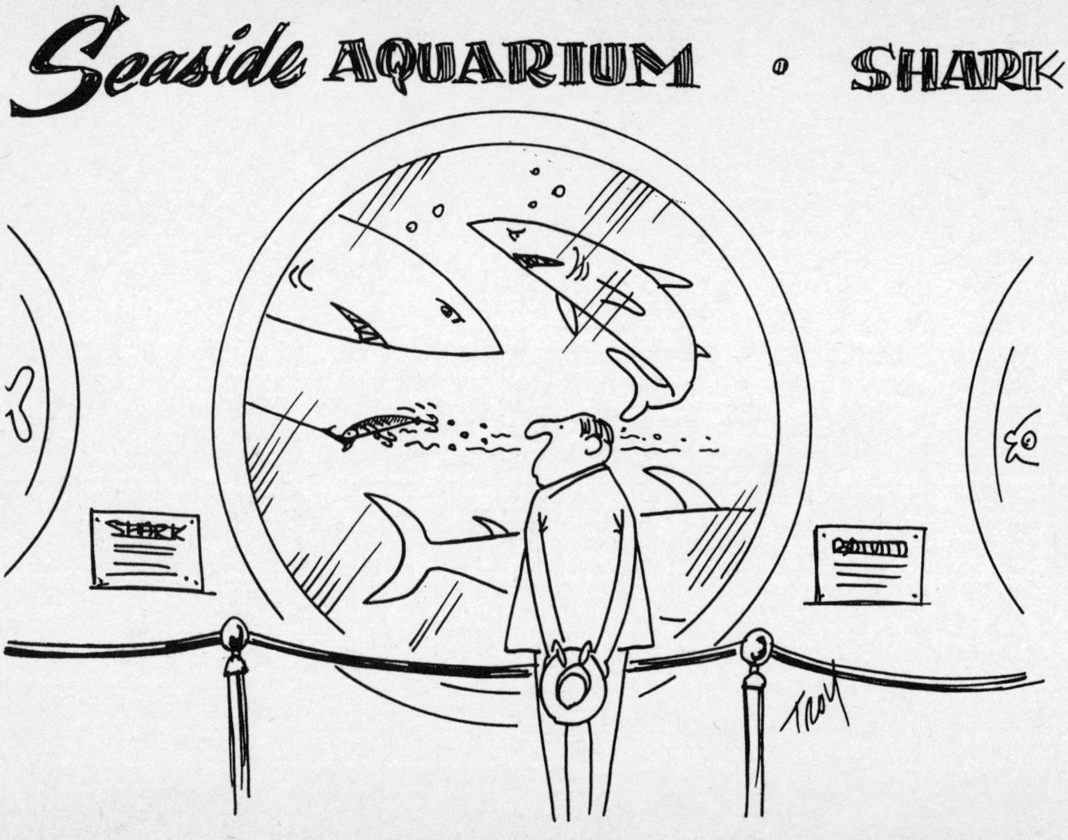
Seaside AQUARIUM · SHARK
SHARK
TROY

"He always seems to remember what's emerging."

"When I said 'Let's see you cast a fly . . .' "

"That guy thinks like a fish."

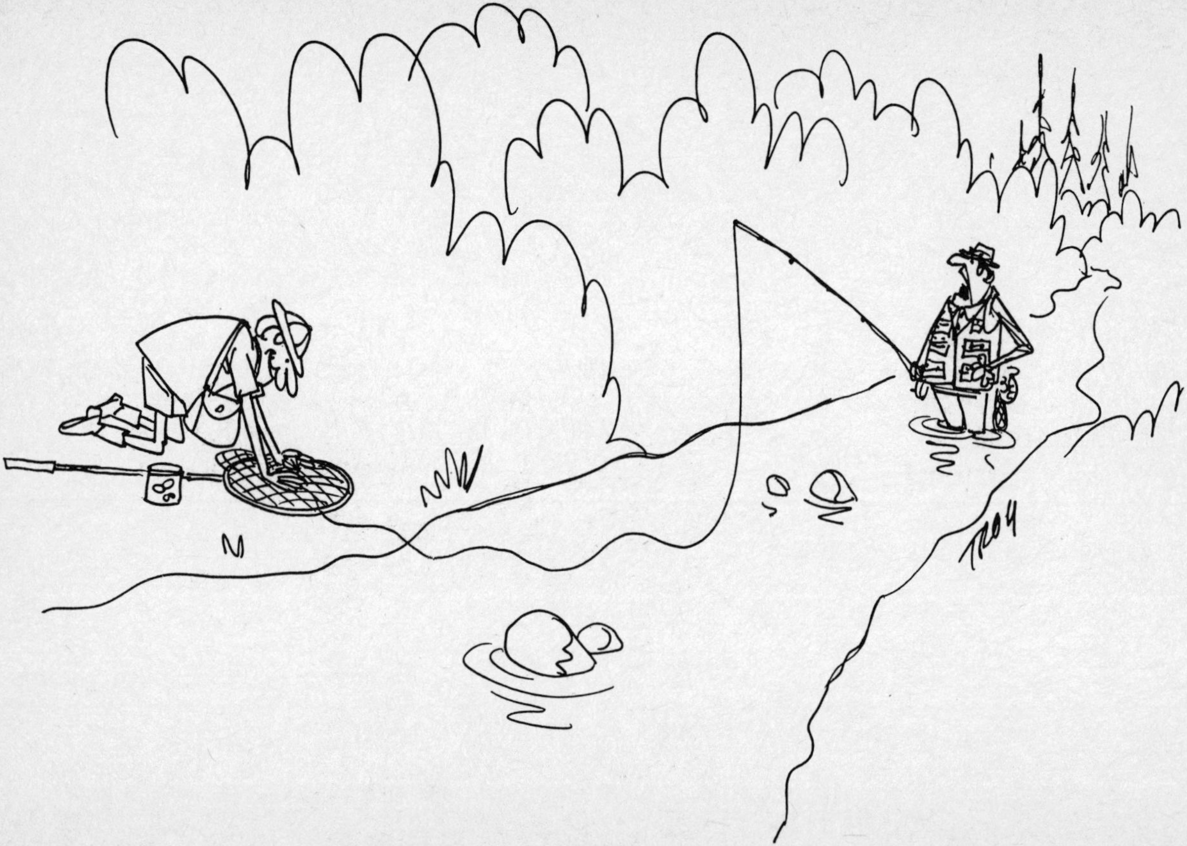

"Hey!"

"That's not exactly what I meant by 'casting a streamer.'"

" . . . BOOMBA YA YA BOOMBA BABY YA YA *click*."

"What I like about this lake is when you get a fish, it's a . . ."

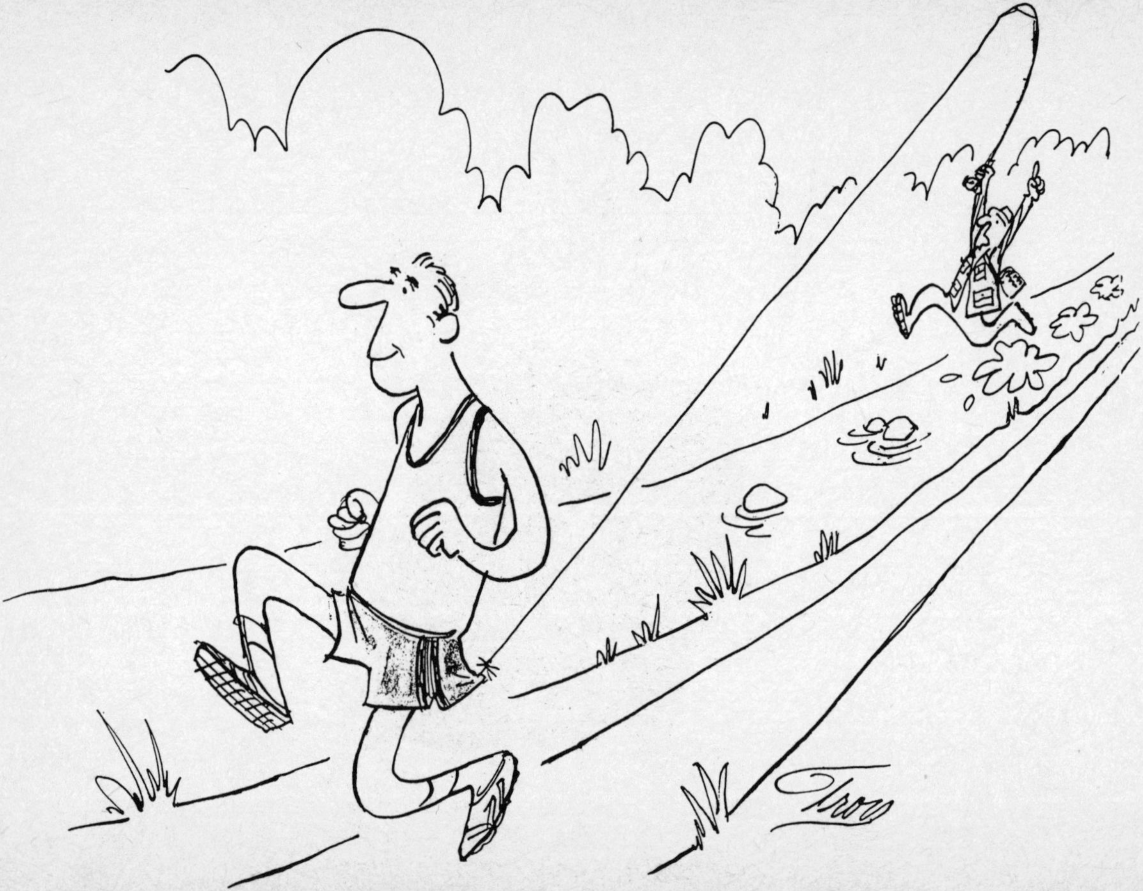

"Good heavens, look at the size of that hatch."

"Some guys are born waders."

"You don't *see* many salmon runs like this one."

"Control yourself, man, it's only a few more days to opening day!"